ISBN 978-0-260-49021-6
PIBN 11123451

FB &c Ltd, Dalton House, 60 Windsor Avenue, London, SW19 2RR.
Company number 08720141. Registered in England and Wales.

S. R. A.—B. A. I. 134. Issue 1 August 6, 1918.

United States Department of Agriculture,

BUREAU OF ANIMAL INDUSTRY.

JOHN R. MOHLER, CHIEF OF BUREAU.

SERVICE AND REGULATORY ANNOUNCEMENTS.

JUNE, 1918.

[This publication is issued monthly for the dissemination of information, instructions, rulings, etc., concerning the work of the Bureau of Animal Industry. Free distribution is limited to persons in the service of the bureau, establishments at which the Federal meat inspection is conducted, public officers whose duties make it desirable for them to have such information, and journals especially concerned. Others desiring copies may obtain them from the Superintendent of Documents, Government Printing Office, Washington, D. C., at 5 cents each, or 50 cents a year. A supply will be sent to each official in charge of a station or branch of the bureau service, who should promptly distribute copies to members of his force. A file should be kept at each station for reference.]

CONTENTS.

DIPLOMACY IN THE FIELD.

By EDWARD HORSTMAN, *Veterinary Inspector.*

[The following article, prepared for a meeting of inspectors engaged in tick eradication, is published for the benefit of employees in that and other branches of the bureau service. Much of what is said is applicable to other kinds of field work, including meat inspection.]

Diplomacy in the field, or diplomacy in any branch of industrial life, is characterized by special tact in the management of affairs. We can not all hope to excel in this quality, because we may not be sufficiently skilled in the art of handling men and affairs, but an inspector in the field has a wonderful range for using good judgment and tact if he will stop to study the man whom he is attempting to prevail upon to dip his cattle.

Use Persuasion First.

There are two sides to tick-eradication work. The mechanical side consists of building vats, making solutions, and dipping cattle; and if there is no opposition to the dipping everything goes along smoothly and satisfactorily. However, where opposition arises there is need of action of some sort. The first impulse is to resort to the law and compel the objector to dip. Some inspectors have a motto of "Dip or affidavit," but that is not the wisest plan to follow in any instance. An inspector who can not differentiate between the obstinate antidipper and the one who merely lacks knowledge of the benefits and necessity of dipping will not prove a success as an inspector. We must not forget that none of us are infallible and that the cattle owner has his own ideas, sometimes peculiar no doubt, but he is entitled to an opinion, and it is one of the duties of the inspector to overcome his false notions against dipping. His opinion should be respected, but he should be told that in justice to himself he should first recognize the facts as regards the ultimate aims of tick eradication and so leave his mind open to conviction before he comes to a final conclusion.

It must be remembered that not so very long ago the southern plantation owner was practically a king on his own plantation, and that feeling in a measure is still present; consequently it is obnoxious to such a man to be told or made to feel that he must do certain things which he considers unnecessary. Compulsion grates on his nerves. So it is wise diplomacy for the inspector to get away from force as far as possible and instead to picture by alluring words the benefits of the eradication of ticks, the upbuilding of the cattle industry, increased prices, and the cessation of dipping when the last tick is gone. Boil down the facts and present them in a simple, unbiased way. Gain the man's confidence, friendship, and respect, and do not fight him.

If there is no hope of converting the objector, then proceed in a businesslike manner to apply the forces of the law at your command without unnecessary fuss. Have your evidence clear and clean-cut; don't go off half-cocked and wonder why you didn't get a verdict. You must bear in mind you are a stranger in a strange land, that the man on trial is among his boyhood friends, and that you yourself must stand well in the community before you can hope for success. The inspector's personal deportment in the community often has a great deal to do with the outcome of cases brought before a jury.

Things That Hinder.

Inspectors sometimes unthinkingly make indiscreet remarks in conversation which are carried to all parts of the county like a wireless message. I know of a case where an inspector inadvertently made a remark in a certain county where everything was going well up to that time, but after that Sherman's famous remark about war was applicable.

Nothing great was ever achieved without enthusiasm. A successful inspector must be enthusiastic; he must be level-headed; he must be energetic. The things that usually hold back tick eradication are the indifferent local inspector (the lazy man), the incompetent local inspector (too old for any use), and the skeptical owner (the "personal liberty" man).

What is this personal liberty? It is the benighted idea of some antidippers who have a total disregard for law and order, and consider that their "personal rights," and not what the statutes provide, should be the law of the land. Such a person is commonly termed a knocker, who always imagines himself a crowd and is usually found at meetings to ask such questions as "What's good for hollow horn?"

The answer to the personal rights man is that he has not only rights but plain duties to perform as well, and that the right sort of man will pay more attention to his duties than he does to his rights.

Emphasize Cooperation.

In talking to a Mississippi audience I laid special stress on cooperation and copartnership in tick eradication, and one very old gray-haired citizen opposed to dipping got up and said: "That reminds me of the story of two men who went into a copartnership on a day's hunt. They were to divide what they got that day. All they killed was a turkey and a buzzard; so when the dividing time came they argued about who should have the turkey; but, you know, in the end someone got that buzzard. And that's the way this tick eradication is going to turn out."

It was incumbent on me to say something, so I said: "You didn't say who got the buzzard in your story, but I'll tell you in my story that the tick has been getting the turkey for years, and there's plenty of evidence that the buzzard is always hovering around the cattle owner whose cattle harbor ticks."

Factors in Successful Work.

Every inspector is a necessary cog in the wheel of tick eradication. He may do much to mar the work, or he may be a powerful help in its prosecution. The greatest success of an inspector depends largely on the ability that he shows in prosecuting the work and in "handling the people." If he knows his business there should be little trouble in gaining the confidence of the cattle owners, and thus his work will be considerably lightened.

All obstinate antidippers should be prosecuted to the fullest extent, yet much hardship can be avoided if a little diplomacy is used.

Success is not obtained by individual efforts alone, but by the cooperation of all concerned in the work.

It has been an arduous and responsible task to mold public sentiment in the South in favor of tick eradication. Had a State-wide campaign been started 10 years ago it would have died from inanition. Only by slow absorption and the diplomatic handling of county by county has the work been crowned with success.

CHANGES IN DIRECTORY.

Meat Inspection Inaugurated.

20-D. Wilson & Co., Inc., and Wilson & Co., 89 South Front Street, Memphis, Tenn.
975. Holland Pure Food Co., 660 Vinewood Avenue, Detroit, Mich.
*265. The Wichita and Oklahoma Serum Co., Twenty-first and Wabash Streets, Wichita, Kans.

Meat Inspection Withdrawn.

73. Wisconsin Packing Co., New Richmond, Wis.
760. Reiland Packing Co., Grand Rapids, Wis.
282. M. Crane Co., New York, N. Y.
214. Statter & Co., Sioux City, Iowa.

Meat Inspection Temporarily Suspended.

627. D. M. Bodine, Trenton, N. J.
122. Oakland Milk Feeding Co., Greeneville, Tenn.
556. Walker Properties Association, Austin, Tex.
939. Royal Packing Co., Kansas City, Kans.
1003. Interstate Vaccine Co., Kansas City, Mo.
113. P. D. Hughes, Camden, N. J.
378-A. Nagle Packing Co., Detroit, Mich.
873. The Stokes-Frantz Canning Co., Denver, Colo.

---

* Conducts slaughtering.

Meat Inspection Reinaugurated Following Suspension.

146. Purity Cross, Inc., 11 Central Avenue, West Orange, N. J.

Change in Name of Establishment.

489. Bronx Provision Co., Inc., 2692–2696 Third Avenue, New York, N. Y., instead of Becker Bros. and Mott Haven Packing House.

Station Added.

West Orange, N. J. (Substation of Newark, N. J.)

Stations Discontinued.

New Richmond, Wis.
Austin, Tex. (Substation of Fort Worth, Tex.)
Greeneville, Tenn. (Substation of Morristown, Tenn.)
Grand Rapids, Wis.

Change of Official in Charge.

Dr. W. F. Osborn instead of Dr. J. I. Martin, Tifton, Ga.

Change of Address of Official in Charge.

Dr. R. G. Rice, P. O. Box 319, Watertown, S. Dak., instead of care South Dakota Packing and Shipping Co., Watertown, S. Dak.

Note.

Waycross, Ga., has been changed from a station to a substation of Moultrie, Ga.

CHANGES IN WORK OF FIELD INSPECTION AND TUBERCULOSIS ERADICATION DIVISIONS.

Effective July 1, 1918, the work of the Field Inspection Division and the Tuberculosis Eradication Division has been rearranged as follows:

The Tuberculosis Eradication Division will devote its entire time to the work relating to the eradication of tuberculosis of animals.

The supervision of the interstate transportation of live stock and the work relating to the enforcement of the 28-hour law, heretofore under the direction of the Tuberculosis Eradication Division but which are allied closely to projects handled by the Field Inspection Division, are transferred to the latter division.

NOTICES REGARDING MEAT INSPECTION.

METAL BRUSHES.

Referring to the use of metal brushes for brushing carcasses and parts and for scrubbing equipment with which meats come into direct contact, it is reliably reported that the points of brushes made of fine or slender steel wire break easily and penetrate or adhere to the meats, and that on account of their small diameter the presence of these broken ends in or on the meat is difficult of detection. Their presence in meats is an element of danger to consumers, particularly where the meats are to be used in the preparation of a chopped or ground product. To insure the elimination of this possible danger proprietors and operators of official establishments are requested to discontinue the use of brushes made of fine or slender wire for brushing meats or scrubbing equipment with which meats come in direct contact. No objection is offered to the use of brushes made of heavy wire or strands which do not break readily and which are too blunt to penetrate the meat easily. However, in all cases where metal brushes are used on meat or equipment inspectors should make careful observations and see that no broken ends are mixed with or left adhering to the meat.

PERMITTED COLORS FOR CASINGS AND FATS.

In order to conform to Food Inspection Decision 175, the bureau will permit any of the following colors or mixtures of these colors to be used for dyeing casings of meat food products or to be added to prepared fats:

(*a*) Annatto and turmeric.

(*b*) Coal-tar colors as follows:

Red shades:

107. Amaranth.
56. Ponceau 3 R.
517. Erythrosine.

Orange shade:

85. Orange I.

Yellow shades:

4. Naphthol yellow S.
94. Tartrazine.
11. Sudan I.
16. Butter yellow.
Yellow A. B. (Benzeneazo-b-naphthylamine).
Yellow O. B. (Ortho-Tolueneazo-b-naphthylamine).

Green shade:

435. Light green S. F. yellowish.

Blue shade:

692. Indigo disulfoacid.

The numbers preceding the names refer to the numbers of the colors as listed in A. G. Green's edition of the Schultz-Julius Systematic Survey of the Organic Coloring Matters, published in 1904.

ANIMALS SLAUGHTERED UNDER FEDERAL MEAT INSPECTION, MAY, 1918.

Station.	Cattle.	Calves.	Sheep.	Goats.	Swine.
Chicago	168,484	84,311	194,237	665	570,729
Fort Worth	35,632	17,325	10,049	6,367	32,628
Kansas City	96,264	13,441	78,846	5,861	264,726
National Stock Yards	43,489	10,920	22,788	84	143,322
Omaha	80,385	5,555	97,970	393	211,974
St. Louis	13,358	2,210	3,557	24	103,201
Sioux City	26,001	3,156	5,647		113,543
South St. Joseph	29,902	3,108	37,880	4	146,405
All other establishments	288,240	217,327	208,089	589	1,505,797
Total: May, 1918	781,755	357,353	659,063	13,987	3,092,325
May, 1917	815,071	344,598	632,451	23,110	3,083,518
11 months ending May, 1918	10,108,725	3,010,720	8,032,199	131,698	32,666,056
11 months ending May, 1917	8,455,321	2,403,244	10,633,387	163,496	37,526,003

IMPORTS OF FOOD ANIMALS AND OF MEATS AND MEAT FOOD PRODUCTS.

The statements following show the imports of food animals and of meats and meat food products inspected by the Bureau of Animal Industry during May, 1918, with figures for other periods for comparison.

Imports of food animals.

Country of export.	Cattle.	Swine.	Sheep.	Goats.
Mexico	15,823		3,844	1,903
Canada	7,698	49	59	
Great Britain	328		5	
Total: May, 1918	23,849	49	3,908	1,903
May, 1917	27,025	160	220	226
11 months ending May, 1918	267,019	13,638	151,620	23,789
11 months ending May, 1917	340,613	2,849	154,380	20,142

Imports of meats and meat food products.

Country of export.	Fresh and refrigerated.		Canned and cured.	Other products.	Total weight.
	Beef.	Other.			
	Pounds.	*Pounds.*	*Pounds.*	*Pounds.*	*Pounds.*
Argentina			799,344	46,547	845,891
Australia				86,423	86,423
Canada	303,475	462,877	28,489	18,081	812,922
Uruguay			1,034,906	87,357	1,122,263
Other countries	438,164		35,720	66,158	540,042
Total: May, 1918	741,639	462,877	1,898,459	304,566	3,407,541
May, 1917	114,744	1,380,016	470,345	170,117	2,135,222
11 months ending May, 1918	17,240,624	5,381,559	21,601,099	11,209,611	55,432,893
11 months ending May, 1917	14,827,880	4,828,975	3,076,111	1,037,906	23,770,872

Condemned in May, 1918: Beef, 44,447 pounds; veal, 360 pounds; pork, 7,151 pounds; total, 51,958 pounds.
Refused entry: Pork, 237,674 pounds.

FOREIGN OFFICIALS AUTHORIZED TO SIGN INSPECTION CERTIFICATES FOR MEAT AND PRODUCTS FOR IMPORTATION INTO THE UNITED STATES.

The following are additional names, addresses, and facsimile signatures of foreign national Government officials authorized to sign and issue certificates of inspection for meat and meat food products offered for importation into the United States:

Country, name, and address.	Signature.
Brazil.	
Martinho de Lima Guimaraes, Rosario, Rio Grande do Sul.	
Canada.	
J. W. Smith, Edmonton, Alberta.	
J. H. Burnet, Edmonton, Alberta.	
D. A. Currie, Winnipeg, Manitoba.	
J. Douglas Hogan, Winnipeg, Manitoba.	
Paraguay.	
Julio A. Salcedo.	(The address and facsimile signature will be published later.)

INSPECTION AND TESTING OF ANIMALS FOR CANADA.

The following changes have been made in the list of practicing veterinarians registered by the bureau and authorized to inspect and test with mallein horses, mules, and asses intended for export to Canada:

Name Added to List.

H. T. Graves, Puyallup, Wash.

Names Removed from List.

C. O. Kroener, Chicago, Ill.
Edward Pugh, Lawton, Okla.

TEXAS-FEVER QUARANTINE—REVISED LIST OF PLACES TO WHICH SOUTHERN CATTLE MAY BE SHIPPED FOR IMMEDIATE SLAUGHTER.

State and Federal permission has been granted for the shipment of southern cattle for immediate slaughter to the following-named places:

District of Columbia: Benning Union Stock Yards.

Florida: *Jacksonville,* Interstate Stock Yard Co. (Armour & Co.); Jacksonville Cattle Co.

Illinois: *Cairo,* E. Bucher Packing Co.; *Chicago,* Union Stock Yards Co.; *East St. Louis,* East Side Packing Co.; *National Stock Yards,* St. Louis National Stock Yards Co.; *Peoria,* Wilson Provision Co.; *Springfield,* Franz Brothers Packing Co.

Indiana: *Indianapolis,* Brown Brothers, Indianapolis Union Stock Yards Co.; Kingan & Co.; The Indianapolis Abattoir Co.; *Muncie,* Kuhner Packing Co.

Iowa: *Ottumwa,* John Morell & Co.; *Sioux City,* The Cudahy Packing Co.

Kansas: *Frontenac,* Menghini Bros. Packing Co.; *Kansas City,* Kansas City Stock Yards Co.; *Pittsburg,* Hull & Dillon Packing Co.; *Wichita,* Wichita Union Stock Yards Co.

Kentucky: *Louisville,* Bourbon Stock Yards Co.

Louisiana: *New Orleans,* Crescent City Stock Yards and Slaughter House Co., New Orleans Butchers Cooperative Abattoir Associations; *Shreveport,* Shreveport Packing Co.

Maryland: *Baltimore,* Union Stock Yards.

Massachusetts: *Brighton,* Brighton Abattoir Co.; *Somerville,* New England Dressed Meat & Wool Co., Sturtevant and Haley Beef & Supply Co.

Michigan: *Detroit,* Hammond, Standish & Co., W. J. Kamman, Kamman Beef Co., Mason Beef Co., Michigan Beef Co., Michigan Central Stock Yards Co., Newton Beef Co., Parker-Webb & Co., Sullivan Packing Co., W. B. Thompson.

Missouri: *Kansas City,* Kansas City Stock Yards Co.; *St. Louis,* Carondelet Packing Co., Independent Stock Yards Co., St. Louis Independent Packing Co., Swift & Co.; *Sedalia,* Stephenson Packing Co.; *South St. Joseph,* St. Joseph Stock Yards Co., Freund Packing Co.

Nebraska: *South Omaha,* Union Stock Yards Co.

New Jersey: *Camden,* D. D. Helm; *Jersey City,* (Harsimus), Armour & Co.; *Newark* (Kearny), Swift & Co.

New York: *Buffalo,* East Buffalo Stock Yards Co., Jacob Dold Packing Co., C. Klinck Packing Co.; *New York,* Armour & Co., Moe Frank, New York Butchers' Dressed Meat Co., Joseph Stern & Sons, Strauss & Adler, Sulzberger & Sons Co., Swift & Co., United Dressed Beef Co.

North Carolina: *Wilmington,* Carolina Packing Co.

OHIO: *Ashtabula*, F. C. Gerald; *Cincinnati*, Cincinnati Abattoir Co.; *Cleveland*, Blumenstock Reid Co., Cleveland Provision Co., Nick Davis, John Deobald, Eisenman Bros., J. J. Flick Dressed Beef Co., Hartman Provision Co., Hughes Provision Co., Koblenxer Bros., Lake Erie Provision Co., Long Dressed Beef Co., Ohio Provision Co., Retail Butchers' Protective Association, Teufel Bros., Theurer-Norton Provision Co., Henry Walcher, Webb Bros.; *West Mentor*, F. E. Presley; *West Toledo* N. Rassel Sons Co., Stautzenbach, Bowers & Taylor.

OKLAHOMA: *Oklahoma*, Oklahoma National Stock Yards.

PENNSYLVANIA: *Allentown*, Arbogast & Bastian Co.; *Altoona*, United Home Dressed Meat Co.; *Butler*, Butler Beef & Provision Co.; *Chester*, John J. Buckley Co.; *Coatesville*, Shallcross & Son; *Erie*, Hiabach Bros., Killmaier & Co., Schaffner Bros.; *Harrisburg*, Brelsford Packing & Storage Co.; *Johnstown*, Armour & Co.; *Lancaster*, Lancaster Stock Yards; *McKeesport*, Peters Packing Co.; *Mount Carmel*, L. W. Weissinger & Bros.; *Philadelphia*, Armour & Co., Consolidated Dressed Beef Co., D. B. Martin & Co., West Philadelphia Stock Yard Co.; *Philipsburg*, Philipsburg Beef Co.; *Pittsburgh*, Armour & Co., Dunlevy Packing Co., Pittsburg Provision & Packing Co., Rea & Co., Swift & Co., Union Stock Yards Co.; *Punxsutawney*, Punxsutawney Beef & Provision Co.; *Reading*, Reading Abattoir Co.; *Scranton*, Frank Carr, Stowers Pork Packing & Provision Co.; *Shamokin*, Croninger Packing Co.; *Washington*, E. J. Young Packing Co.; *Williamsport*, Williamsport Packing Co., John Peters.

TENNESSEE: *Chattanooga*, J. H. Allison & Co.

TEXAS: *El Paso*, Peyton Packing Co.; *Fort Worth*, Fort Worth Stock Yards Co.

VIRGINIA: *Danville*, A. Greenberg; *Norfolk*, Banks Bros., Union Stock Yards Co.; *Richmond*, Richmond Union Stock Yards, Valentine's Meat Juice Co.

WEST VIRGINIA: *Wheeling*, F. Schenk & Sons Co.

WISCONSIN: *Cudahy*, Cudahy Bros.; *Milwaukee*, Plankinton Packing Co.

LICENSES FOR VETERINARY BIOLOGICAL PRODUCTS.

The following changes have been made in the list of licenses for the manufacture of veterinary biological products for the year 1918 under the act of Congress of March 4, 1913 (37 Stat., 832), and the regulations made thereunder (B. A. I. Order 196):

Licenses Issued.

License No.	Date.	Name and address of firm.	Products.
	1918.		
3	June 13	H. K. Mulford Co., Glen Olden, Pa.	Antiblackleg serum, antibotulinus serum.
17	June 21	Beebe Laboratories (Inc.), 161-163 West Third Street, St. Paul, Minn.	Swine-plague vaccine.
21	June 15	Continental Serum Laboratories Co., Isette Avenue and Bidwell Street, Muscatine, Iowa.	Anti-hog-cholera serum; hog-cholera virus.
39-A	June 1	Purity Biological Laboratories, Chambers and Chicago Streets, Sioux City, Iowa.	Blackleg filtrate.

License Canceled.

License No. 117, Kansas Blackleg Serum Co., Wichita, Kans., issued December 28, 1917, was canceled June 22, 1918.

COLLECTION OF ANTI-HOG-CHOLERA SERUM.

The following ruling is made with regard to the production of anti-hog-cholera serum at establishments licensed under the act of March 4, 1913 (37 Stat., 832):

Anti-hog-cholera serum shall be derived only from hyperimmune hogs which have been subjected to not more than four successive bleedings after hyperimmunization.

The first bleeding shall take place not earlier than 10 days after hyperimmunization; subsequent bleedings shall not take place more frequently than once in 7 days, and the last bleeding shall be made on a date not later than 38 days after hyperimmunization.

TEST FOR PURITY AND POTENCY OF ANTI-HOG-CHOLERA SERUM.

The following instructions supersede those given under the foregoing title in Service and Regulatory Announcements for June, 1917, pages 74–76:

All anti-hog-cholera serum which has been prepared and mixed in accordance with outstanding bureau orders and requirements shall be tested by licensed establishments for purity and potency in the following described manner:

SECTION 1. *Paragraph 1.*—For use in testing each batch of 100,000 c. c. of anti-hog-cholera serum or less, 7 healthy pigs, susceptible to hog cholera, and weighing not less than 45 pounds and not more than 90 pounds each, shall be furnished by the establishment.

Paragraph 2.—Each of the 7 pigs furnished for the test shall be injected with 2 c. c. of hog-cholera virus; of these pigs, 5 shall receive 20 c. c. of the serum which is to be tested. Two of the pigs shall receive no serum and shall serve as controls. The virus and serum injections shall be made simultaneously, the virus being injected into the left and the serum into the right axillary space. The same virus shall be used for the inoculation of all pigs in the test and shall be administered by a veterinary inspector.

Paragraph 3.—A veterinary inspector shall indicate the pigs which shall receive serum with virus and those which shall receive the virus only in each serum test.

Paragraph 4.—Pigs which are injected with serum in serum tests shall be held under the observation of a veterinary inspector for a period of 21 days, or as much longer as the inspector in charge may deem necessary to determine the health of the animals and the purity and potency of the serum under test.

Paragraph 5.—Pigs in serum tests which receive virus only shall be held under the observation of a veterinary inspector and shall not be killed unless and until released by a veterinary inspector who shall be satisfied that the pigs are visibly sick of hog cholera, as described in Rule D, paragraph 2, section 2, of this order.

SECTION 2. *Paragraph 1.*—The following principle and rules are declared for a guide in judging the results of serum tests:

Principle.—It is practically impossible in many cases to differentiate accurately between hog cholera, pneumonia, and other conditions affecting hogs without the aid of an autopsy as well as applied laboratory technique and certain experiments which may be necessary to determine the causative agent responsible for the condition. Therefore, when healthy pigs are selected for testing anti-hog-cholera serum any abnormal condition which may arise in the pigs subsequent to their inoculation should be regarded as due either to the virus used or, in the case of the serum-treated pigs, to the fact that the serum does not protect, unless the condition is definitely known or can be shown to be due to some other cause.

Paragraph 2.—The following rules shall be observed in disposing of anti-hog-cholera serum which has been subjected to the tests prescribed by this order:

Rule A.—A serum test shall be declared "no test" if any one of the following conditions obtains:

1. When any of the serum-treated test pigs or both of the control pigs become visibly sick on or before the fourth day after the time of inoculation.

2. When both of the control pigs do not become visibly sick of hog cholera at some time during the test period.

3. When one or both of the control pigs do not become visibly sick of hog cholera within seven days after the time of inoculation.

4. When one or both of the control pigs become visibly sick of hog cholera within 7 days, but do not become visibly sick to a degree sufficient to result in death within 15 days after the time of inoculation.

5. When any of the serum-treated test pigs develop during the test period symptoms of any infectious, contagious, or communicable disease, other than hog cholera, which appears not to have been caused by the serum used.

Rule B.—A serum test shall be declared "unsatisfactory and the serum contaminated" when the following condition obtains:

1. When any of the serum-treated test pigs develop during the test period symptoms of any infectious, contagious, or communicable disease, other than hog cholera, which is known to be due to the serum used.

Rule C.—A serum test shall be declared "unsatisfactory" when any one of the following conditions obtains:

1. When both of the control pigs react as described in Rule D and one of the serum-treated pigs becomes visibly sick subsequent to the fourth day after the time of inoculation and is found not to have fully recovered before the test animals are released by a veterinary inspector, as provided in paragraph 4, section 1, of this order.

2. When both of the control pigs react as described in Rule D and two or more of the serum-treated pigs become visibly sick subsequent to the fourth day after the time of inoculation.

3. When an abscess which is not definitely known to be due to a cause other than the serum used develops at the site of the serum inoculations in any of the serum-treated pigs.

Rule D.—A serum test shall be declared "satisfactory" when the following conditions obtain:

When both of the control pigs become visibly sick of hog cholera at some time during the test period, or when one of them becomes visibly sick subsequent to the fourth day of this period but within 7 days after the test is inaugurated, and visibly sick to a degree sufficient to result in death within 15 days after the time of inoculation, while all of the serum-treated pigs remain well throughout the test, or not more than one of these pigs becomes visibly sick subsequent to the fourth day after the time of inoculation, and fully recovers before the test animals are released by a veterinary inspector as provided in paragraph 4, section 1, of this order.

SECTION 3. *Paragraph 1.*—Anti-hog-cholera serum may be released for marketing as hereinafter prescribed when the test required by this order is found to be "satisfactory" as defined in Rule D, provided the product is recommended for use in doses not less than those appearing in the following table. This table shall be a part of trade labels, wrappers, etc., affixed to or used in connection with each immediate or true container of the product.

	c. c.
For sucking pigs	20
For pigs weighing—	
20 to 40 pounds	30
40 to 90 pounds	35
90 to 120 pounds	45
120 to 150 pounds	55
150 to 180 pounds	65
180 pounds and over	75

As stockyard exposure is considered to be the most dangerous, the doses recommended in amendment 3 to B. A. I. Order 245 are slightly greater than the foregoing.

Paragraph 2.—Anti-hog-cholera serum, the test of which has proved it to be "unsatisfactory" as defined in Rule C of this order may be tested again as hereinbefore described. Should the second test prove to be "satisfactory" as defined in Rule D, the serum may be released for marketing under the conditions detailed above. If the test is again found "unsatisfactory" for the same reason as before, the serum shall not be marketed unless it is refined and tested in accordance with methods approved by the chief of the bureau.

SECTION 4. *Paragraph 1.*—When ordinary defibrinated-blood anti-hog-cholera serum is refined so that its volume is reduced 20 per cent or more, and it is desired to market the product in doses smaller than those indicated above, it shall be tested as aforesaid, except that each pig in the test shall receive 15 c. c. of the product to be tested.

Paragraph 2.—Should this test be found "satisfactory" as defined in Rule D, the product may be marketed, provided it is recommended for use in doses not less than those appearing in the following table. This table shall be a part of trade labels, wrappers, etc., affixed to or used in connection with each immediate or true container of the product.

	c. c.
For sucking pigs	15
For pigs weighing—	
20 to 40 pounds	25
40 to 90 pounds	30
90 to 120 pounds	35
120 to 150 pounds	45
150 to 180 pounds	50
180 pounds and over	60

RESULTS OF PROSECUTIONS FOR VIOLATIONS OF LAWS.

Penalties have been imposed in prosecutions for violations of regulatory laws, as reported to the bureau, as follows:

Live-Stock Quarantine Laws.

Georgia & Florida Railway Co. (2 cases), interstate shipment of cattle in violation of Texas-fever regulations, $200 fine and $24.75 costs.

St. Louis, Iron Mountain & Southern Railway Co. (2 cases), interstate shipment of cattle in violation of Texas-fever regulations, $200 fine and $27.76 costs.

Chicago, Rock Island & Gulf Railway Co. (2 cases), interstate shipment of cattle in violation of Texas-fever regulations, $200 fine and $19.20 costs.

Twenty-Eight-Hour Law.

Central Railroad Co. of New Jersey, $100 fine and $15.15 costs.

Kansas City Southern Railway Co., $100 fine and $13.40 costs.

Southern Railway Co. (2 cases), $200 fine and $20.40 costs.

New York Central Railroad Co., $100 fine and $13.96 costs.

James W. Lusk, receiver St. Louis & San Francisco Railroad Co. (3 cases), $200 fine and 43.67 costs.

B. F. Bush, receiver St. Louis, Iron Mountain & Southern Railway Co., $100 fine and $19.81 costs.

APPOINTMENT OF MEN OF DRAFT AGE TO BE AVOIDED WHEN POSSIBLE.

The attention of employees concerned in the selection of persons for appointment to positions in the bureau is called to the following instructions issued by the Secretary of Agriculture under date of June 3, 1918, with regard to men subject to draft for military service:

We should exhaust every resource to secure the requisite forces before any men within the draft age are called into the service. No man of draft age should be added to the service unless the work to which it is proposed to assign him is essential and urgent and it has been fully and completely demonstrated that no other man can be secured to do the task in reasonably satisfactory fashion. In no event should any indication whatever be given to any such contemplated appointee that his deferred classification may be requested.

EMPLOYEES ENTERING MILITARY OR NAVAL SERVICE.

The attention of inspectors and others in charge is again called to the importance of furnishing the bureau with a full report in each case in which a regular employee enters the military or naval service. In many instances inspectors in charge have failed to comply with the instructions in Service and Regulatory Announcements for February, 1918, page 14, relative to this matter, thus causing considerable unnecessary correspondence.

Temporary employees are not entitled to military leave. When a temporary employee leaves the bureau service his formal resignation should be obtained before his departure.

In all cases of separation from the service by resignation the reasons for the resignation should be given.

All persons who have entered the service through civil-service examination and certification are entitled to military leave, and when an employee of that kind enters the military service his application for indefinite leave without pay should be obtained before he leaves his work.

An application for military leave should contain a statement showing the branch of the service the applicant expects to enter, such, for example, as the Officers' Reserve Corps, the National Army by draft, the Army, the Navy, or the Marine Corps by voluntary enlistment, the National Guard, or the Naval Militia. If an employee is going into the service in a quasi military capacity, such as military clerk, that fact should be stated.

Whenever possible the military address of the person leaving the bureau service should be given.

Permanent employees who enter the military service should be granted the unused portion of the annual leave to which they are entitled for the current calendar year, provided that their bureau salary and military salary combined do not exceed the rate of $2,000 per annum. In forwarding applications for leave without pay allowance should be made for annual leave under this provision.

The report of an employee about to enter the military or naval service should show the rate of pay that he will receive on the military roll and the date his name was placed on such roll in a pay status.

To facilitate the prompt settlement of salary it is suggested that when an employee enters the military or naval service the salary due him for service in the bureau be claimed on a separate voucher (Form 3), with the required report, application for indefinite leave, and time report securely fastened thereto.

Should employees enter the military or naval service after the monthly pay roll has been submitted the bureau should be notified by telegraph that the employee "has been drafted" or "has enlisted as a private" or "has accepted a commission," as the case may be, giving the last day he worked in the bureau's service and the date his military pay began, with rate of pay.

USE OF TRANSPORTATION REQUESTS UNDER ORDER OF THE UNITED STATES RAILROAD ADMINISTRATION.

Memorandum No. 241, issued by the Secretary of Agriculture June 8, 1918, provides as follows:

Section 10 of General Order No. 28 ("Increased Freight and Passenger Rates"), issued on May 25, 1918, by the Director General of the United States Railroad Administration, becomes effective June 10, 1918, and reads as follows:

"Passengers traveling in standard sleeping cars and parlor cars shall be required to pay an additional passage charge of sixteen and two-thirds ($16\frac{2}{3}$) per cent of the normal one-way fare, and passengers traveling in tourist sleeping cars an additional passage charge of eight and one-third ($8\frac{1}{3}$) per cent of the normal one-way fare. The foregoing charges are in addition to those required for the occupancy of berths in sleeping cars or seats in parlor cars."

To comply with the provisions of this section, pending appropriate modification of the existing form of transportation requests, it will be necessary for an employee of the Department of Agriculture, when traveling on official business, to issue three transportation requests in connection with each journey involving the use of standard or tourist sleeping car, or parlor car accommodations. The first request will be drawn on the railroad company as heretofore for the ordinary fare at tariff rates. The second request, to cover the sleeping car or parlor car accommodations, will be drawn as heretofore upon the company furnishing these accommodations. The third request, for the additional charge specified in section 10, will be drawn upon the railroad company issuing the transportation on the first request. It will be necessary for the traveler, in drawing this third request, to insert the appropriate phrase from those indicated below:

1. If the travel involves the use of standard sleeping car accommodations, the words "For additional fare for travel in standard sleeping car" will be inserted.
2. If the travel involves the use of a tourist sleeping car, the words "For additional fare for travel in tourist sleeping car" will be inserted.
3. If the travel involves the use of a parlor car or chair car, the words "For additional fare for travel in parlor car" will be inserted.

The inserted matter should be placed in the blank space immediately above the signature and title of the officer countersigning the request; in all other respects the third request will be prepared in the same manner as the first request.

PUBLICATIONS IN JUNE.

[The bureau keeps no general mailing list for sending publications to individual employees. When a new publication is issued one or more copies are usually sent to each officer in charge of a station. If additional copies are desired for distribution to members of the force or for other use they will be sent on request if possible. Individual employees who wish to obtain any of the publications listed here should apply first to the local officer in charge. If he has no extra copies, application may then be made to the Washington office.]

Yearbook Separate 754. Breeding Horses for the United States Army. By H. H. Reese, Animal Husbandry Division. Pp. 18, pl. 4, figs. 8.

The Candling and Preservation of Eggs. Pp. 4, fig. 1. (Leaflet G-25, A. H. Series.)

Destruction of Tetanus Antitoxin by Chemical Agents. By W. N. Berg and R. A. Kelser, Pathological Division. In Journal of Agricultural Research, Vol. XIII, No. 10, pp. 471-495. June 5, 1918.

ORGANIZATION OF THE BUREAU OF ANIMAL INDUSTRY.

Chief: JOHN R. MOHLER.
Assistant Chief: ———.
Chief Clerk: CHARLES C. CARROLL.
Editor: JAMES M. PICKENS.
Animal Husbandry Division: GEORGE M. ROMMEL, chief.
Biochemic Division: M. DORSET, chief.
Dairy Division: B. H. RAWL, chief.
Field Inspection Division: A. W. MILLER, chief.
Meat Inspection Division: R. P. STEDDOM, chief.
Miscellaneous Division: A. M. FARRINGTON, chief.
Pathological Division: JOHN S. BUCKLEY, acting chief.
Quarantine Division: RICHARD W. HICKMAN, chief.
Tick Eradication Division: R. A. RAMSAY, chief.
Tuberculosis Eradication Division: J. A. KIERNAN, chief.
Zoological Division: B. H. RANSOM, chief.
Experiment Station: E. C. SCHROEDER, superintendent.
Office of Hog-Cholera Control: O. B. HESS in charge.
Office of Virus-Serum Control: H. J. SHORE in charge.
Office of Accounts: E. J. NEWMYER in charge.
Appointment Section: GEORGE H. RUSSELL in charge.

ADDITIONAL COPIES
OF THIS PUBLICATION MAY BE PROCURED FROM
THE SUPERINTENDENT OF DOCUMENTS
GOVERNMENT PRINTING OFFICE
WASHINGTON, D. C.
AT
5 CENTS PER COPY
SUBSCRIPTION PRICE, 50 CENTS PER YEAR
▽

CPSIA information can be obtained
at www.ICGtesting.com
Printed in the USA
LVHW042231221118
597992LV00017B/343/P

9 780260 490216